Zia Blizz

FAMILY SAFE DARES
GET TO KNOW THEM

Dares to play Platonically

Family Safe Dares from Truth, Dare & Situations

First Published in **December 2024**

ISBN: 978-93-6356-411-4

PUBLISHING MONGERS

+91 9311101365

Distributed by: Watergies

Rules of engagement

- Minimum players : 2; Maximum players : 10; Best played with : 4-5

- With 2 players, you choose either his team or her team, and do whatever your team gets. You can both do the same dares too, if mutually decided, or start over from the other's team

- With more than 2 players, everyone does every dare or how you decide beforehand

- Every player gets to skip a maximum of three dares. NO EXCEPTIONS.

- Go, get to know them without the risk of going too far

Her turn

#1

Give me a creative compliment

His turn

#2

Drink a mystery drink created by me

Her turn

#3

Pretend to be me for five minutes

His turn

#4

Stay a statue until your next turn

Her turn

#5

Pretend to swim on the floor until your next turn

His turn

#6

Say a tongue
twister

#7

Spell your full
name backward

His turn

#8

Let me tickle
you for ten
seconds

Her turn

#9

Let me post a story on WhatsApp

His turn

#10

Bottoms up my drink

Her turn

#11

Keep clapping
until your next
turn

#12

Let me send a
DM from your
Instagram

Her turn

#13

Imitate whatever I do until your next turn

His turn

#14

Show the most embarrassing picture on your phone

Her turn

#15

Show the search history on your phone

His turn

#16

Post a super long status in gibberish

Her turn

#17

Stay handcuffed until your next turn

His turn

#18

Refill the drink of everyone in the room

#19

Let me style
your hair like I
want

His turn

#20

Take a screenshot of your browsing history and send it to everyone in the room

Her turn

#21

Show me a picture of your most cringy outfit

His turn

#22

Laugh like a supervillain

Her turn

#23

Stay blindfolded until the next round

His turn

#24

Try selling a painting to a blind person

Her turn

#25

Try selling a comb to a bald person

His turn

#26

Whisper a secret
to me

Her turn

#27

Let me draw a tattoo with a permanent marker on your back

His turn

#28

Eat something I say without using your hands

#29

Hold your drink with two hands until your next turn

His turn

#30

Stand on one foot until next round

Her turn

#31

Say over and out after every sentence until your next turn

His turn

#32

Start every sentence with a bark until your next turn

Her turn

#33

Go outside and shout - I am going for you. Run.

His turn

#34

Ring the doorbell of a neighbour and run back

#35

Keep your finger
in your mouth
until your next
turn

His turn

#36

Sing all your responses until your next turn

#37

Try to
impersonate
everyone in the
room

#38

Yell out the first word that comes to your mind

#39

Dance like your
life depended on
it for a minute
without music

His turn

#40

Break dance for twenty seconds

Her turn

#41

Keep two ice cubes in your mouth until they melt

His turn

#42

Let me post a
status on your
behalf

Her turn

#43

Only answer yes until your next turn

His turn

#44

Let me go through your phone for one minute

#45

Post a random
baby scan on
social media

His turn

#46

Let me choose your lock screen and you have to keep it for at least a day

Her turn

#47

Speak in a
different accent
until your next
turn

His turn

#48

Wrestle a pillow

#49

Try jumping with
your drink twice
without spilling

His turn

#50

Text someone – You wouldn't believe what happened, and then do not reply to them

Her turn

#51

Do a dramatic catwalk

#52

Let me draw a
tattoo on your
foot with
permanent
marker

Her turn

#53

Take a shower with your clothes on

His turn

#54

Speak in rhymes until your next turn

Her turn

#55

Pose like a model until your next turn

His turn

#56

Fit as many grapes as you can in your mouth

Her turn

#57

Re-enact your
most
embarrassing
photo ever

His turn

#58

Eat a spoon of sugar

Her turn

#59

Photobomb a
picture

His turn

#60

Walk with your shoelaces tied together

Her turn

#61

Refrigerate your soaked shirt and then wear it after the next round

#62

Colour your
front tooth black
with an eyeliner

Her turn

#63

Do a yoga pose

His turn

#64

Slap yourself

#65

Let me playfully
slap you

His turn

#66

Try selling me an item from the bathroom

Her turn

#67

Show me how you sleep on the floor until your next turn

His turn

#68

Sing a paragraph
of your favourite

song

#69

Go outside the room wearing the blindfold and then find your way back

His turn

#70

Try juggling two
objects for
twenty seconds

Her turn

#71

Smell my armpit

#72

Put on a blindfold
and touch
everyone's face in
the room and
guess who's who

Her turn

#73

Put your clothing
on backwards
until your next
turn

His turn

#74

Reply to the
first five
Instagram stories

Her turn

#75

Brush my teeth

His turn

#76

Sit on the floor
until your next
turn

#77

Drink water in a funny way

His turn

#78

Put on a towel
like a cloak until
your next turn

Her turn

#79

Karaoke to a
song of my
choice

His turn

#80

Introduce
yourself for a
minute

Her turn

#81

Poke anyone randomly five times within five minutes

His turn

#82

Call your friend and say - I am right outside your house. Come out.

Her turn

#83

**Pretend to cry
until your next
turn**

His turn

#84

Go sit in the corner facing the wall until your next turn

#85

Try tying your shoelaces with one hand

His turn

#86

Empty out your
wallet or purse
on the table

#87

Show your
favourite picture
of yourself

His turn

#88

Be everyone's waiter until your next turn

#89

Exchange your
shoes with me

His turn

#90

Pretend to shiver
with cold until
your next turn

Her turn

#91

Hop around the room until your next turn

His turn

#92

Keep your eyes closed until your next turn

#93

Brush your teeth
with peanut
butter

#94

Give a personalised insult to everyone in the room

Her turn

#95

FaceTime your
most recent
contact, burp,
then hang up

His turn

#96

Imitate your favourite fictional character

#97

Ask a stranger for relationship advice

His turn

#98

Read your last
text message
out loud

Her turn

#99

Say two honest things about everyone in the room

His turn

#100

Call a random contact for advice on a rash

Her turn

Bonus

Something on your mind

Bonus

Something on your mind